HAZBIN HOTEL

COLORING BOOK

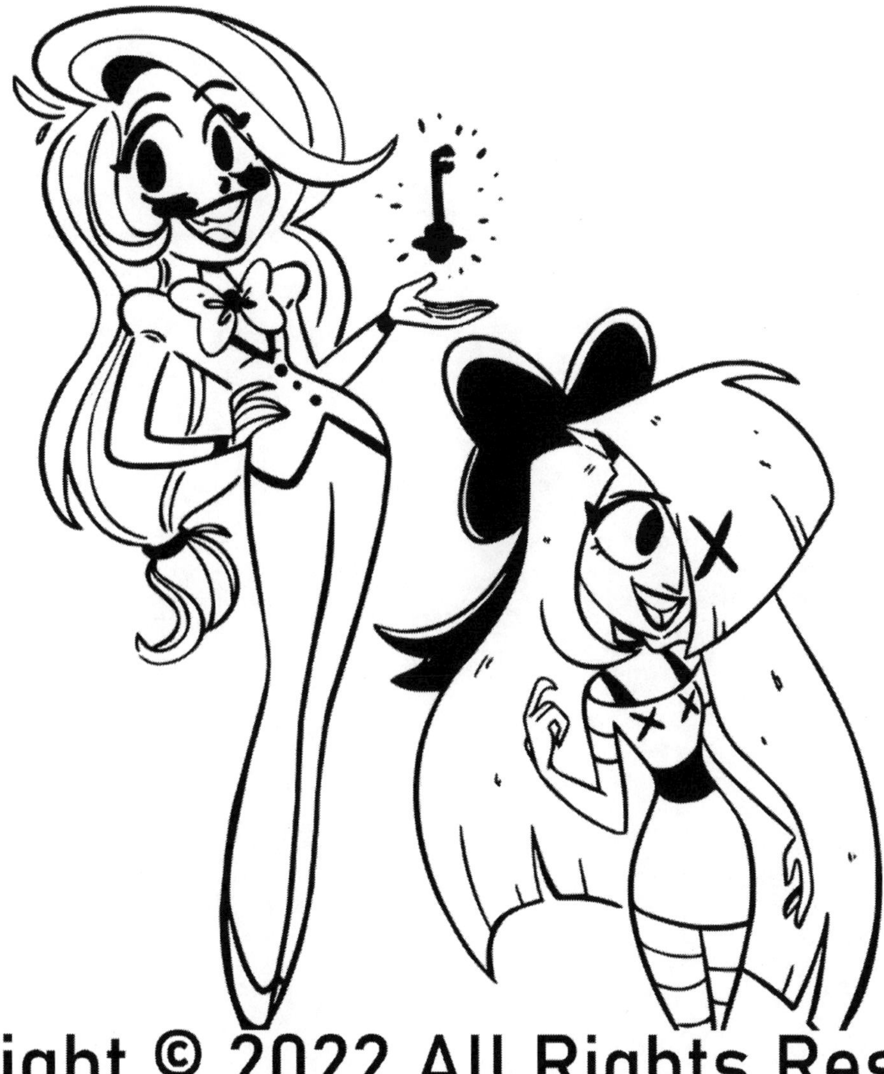

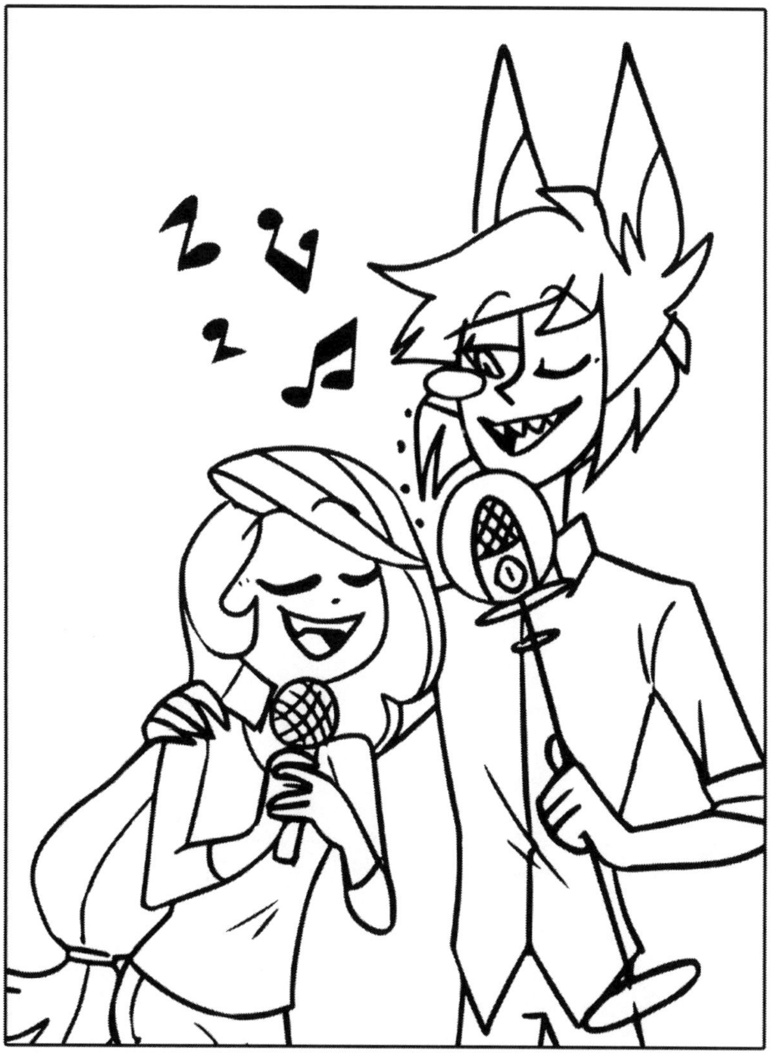

THIS BOOK BELONGS TO

Test Color Page

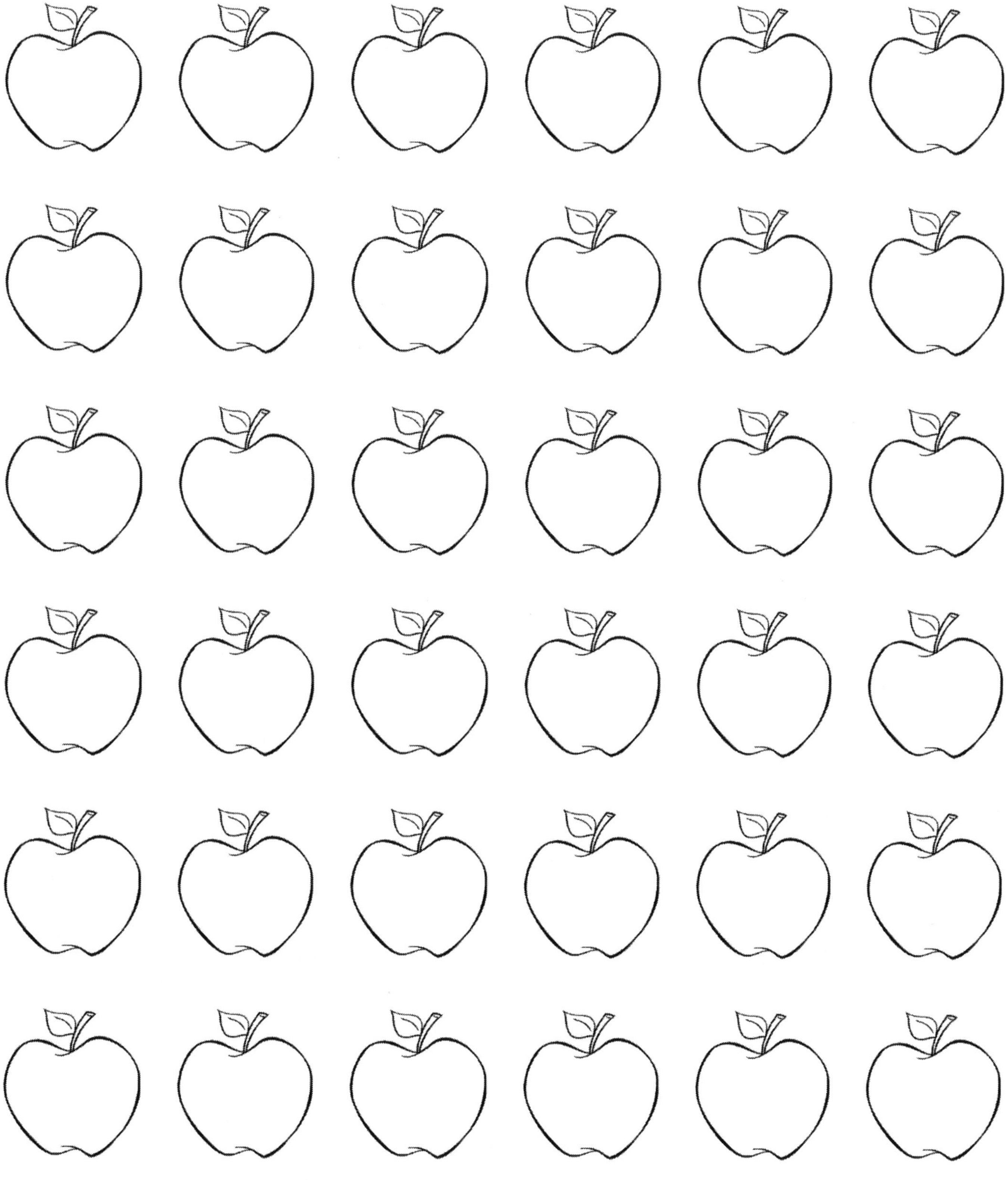

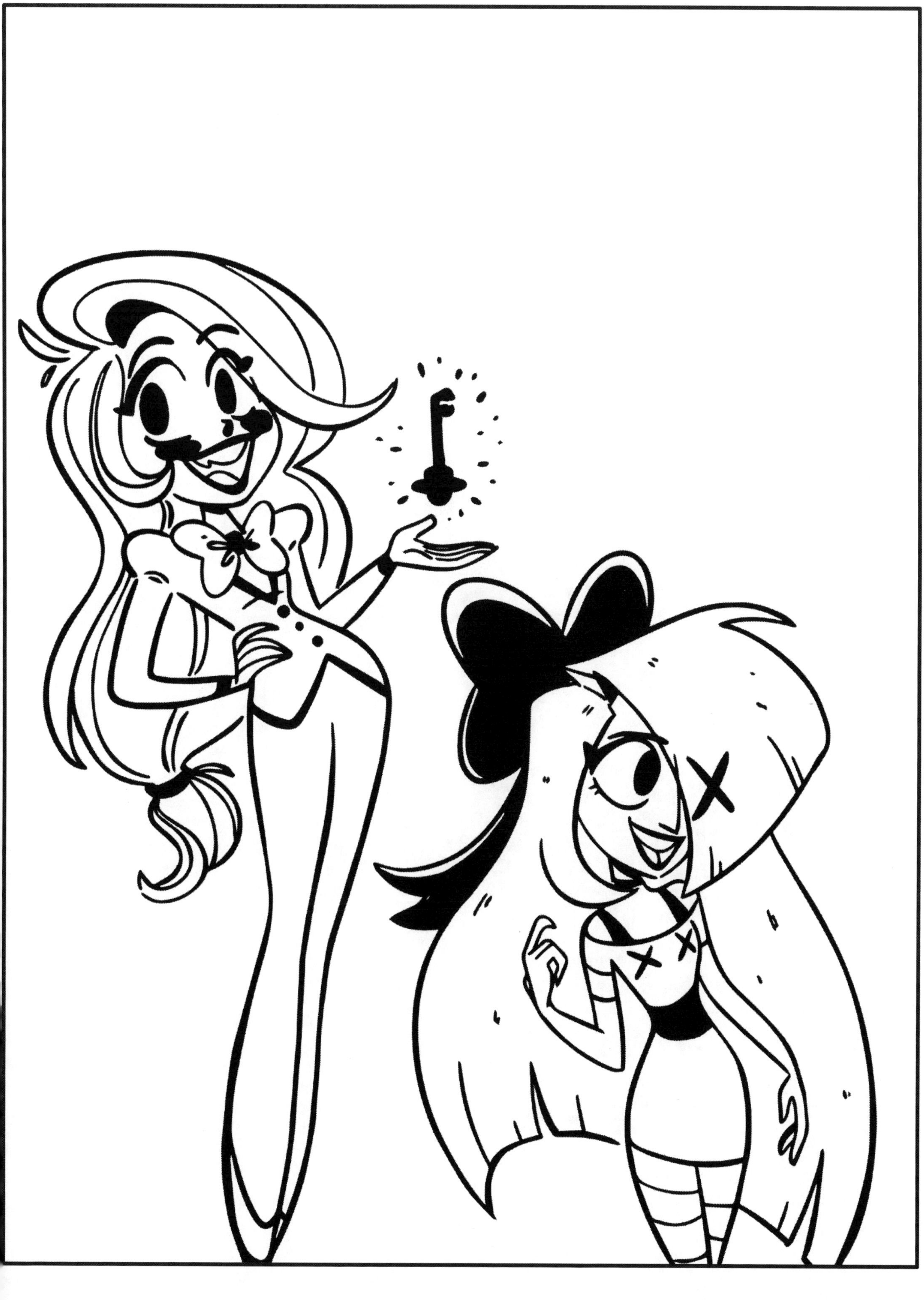

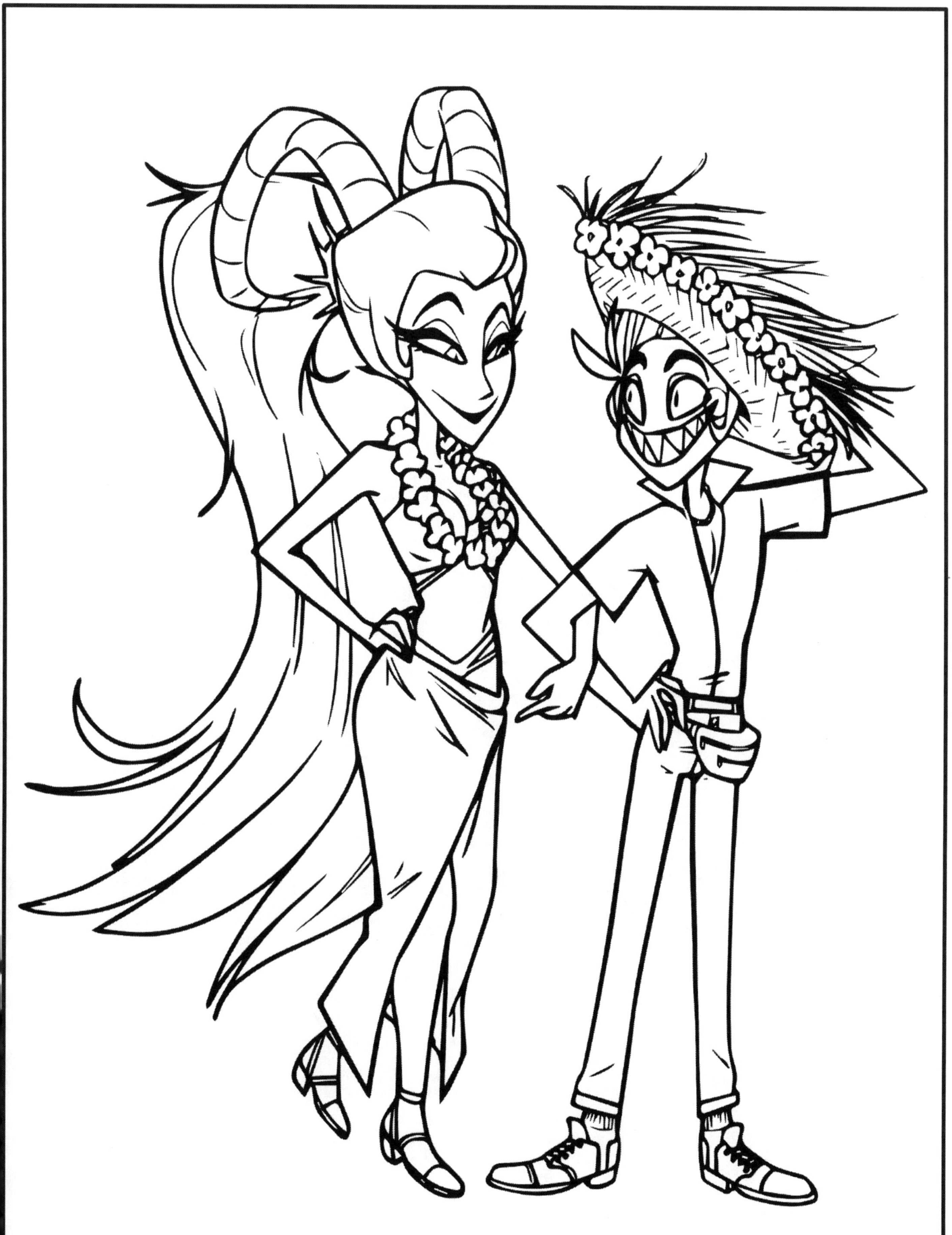

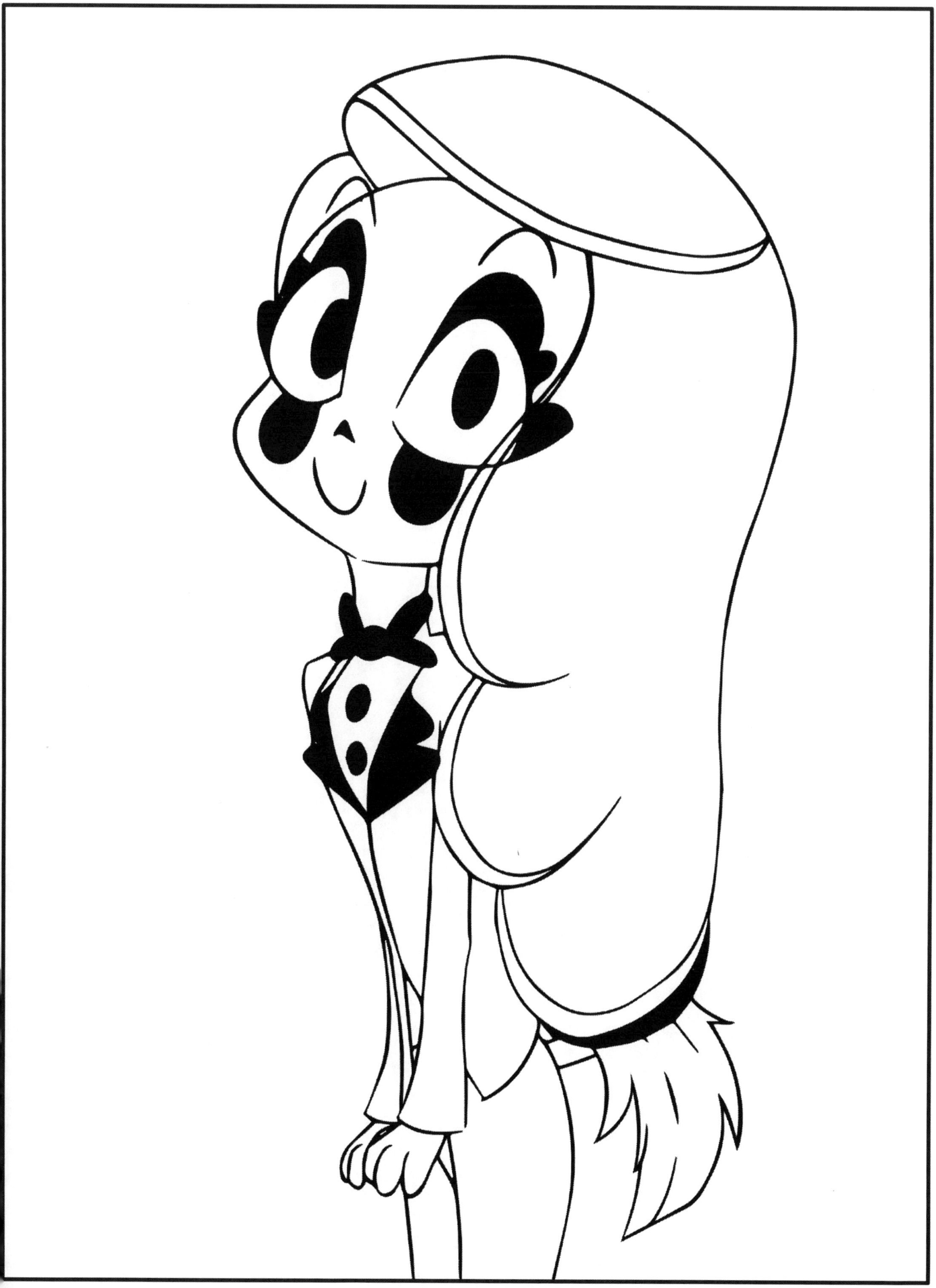

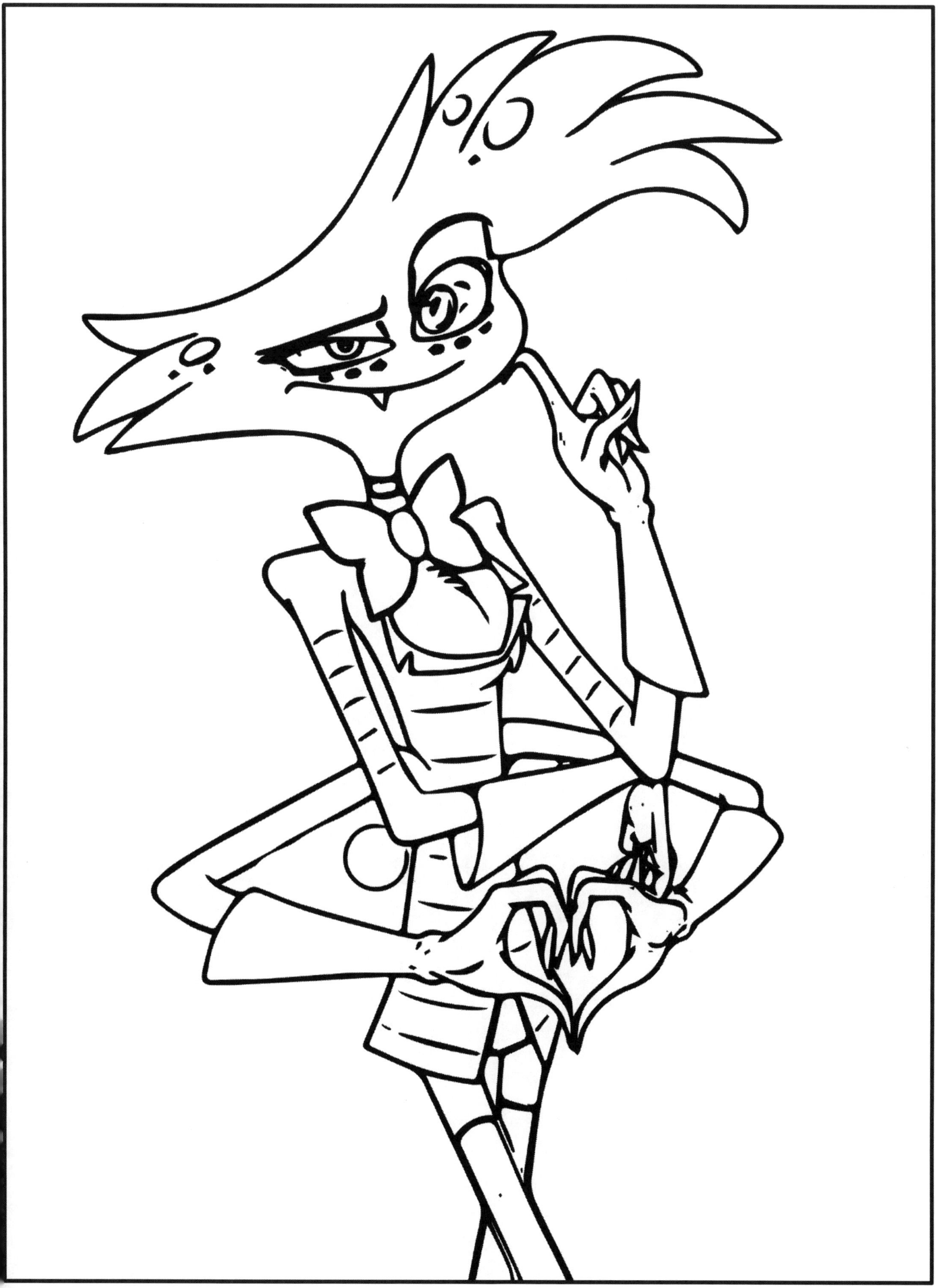

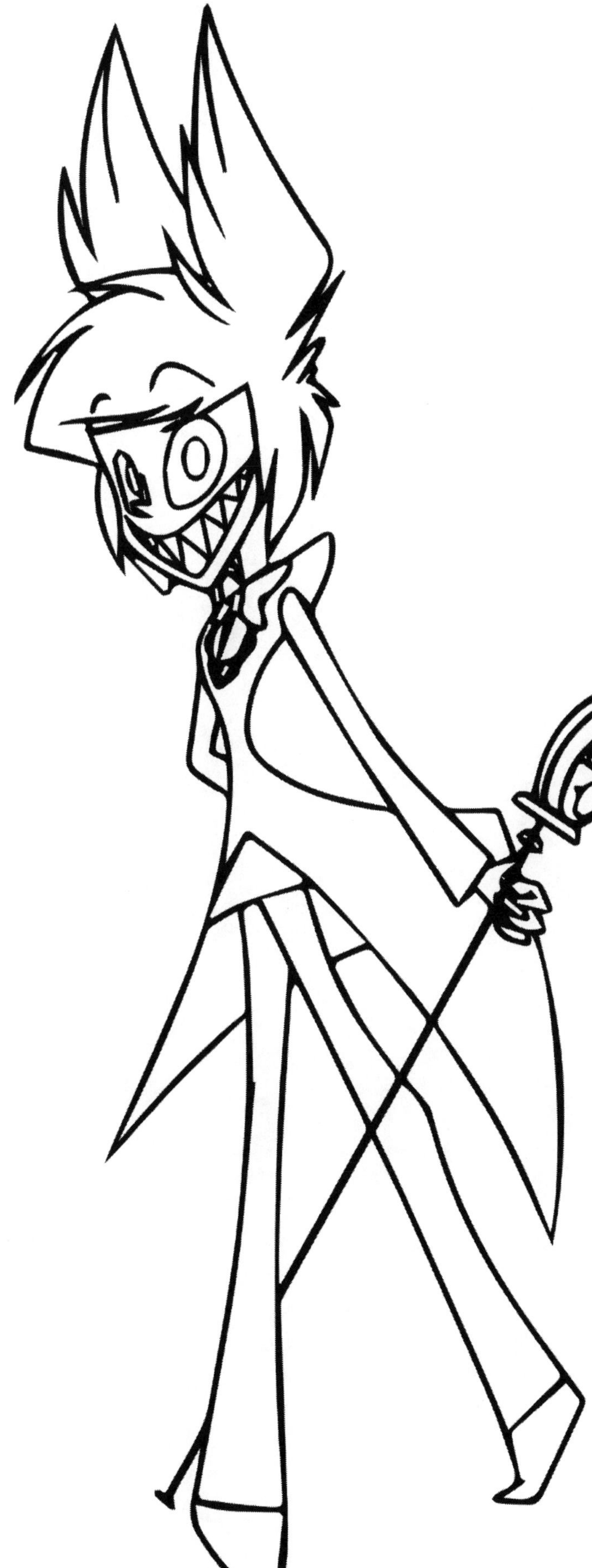

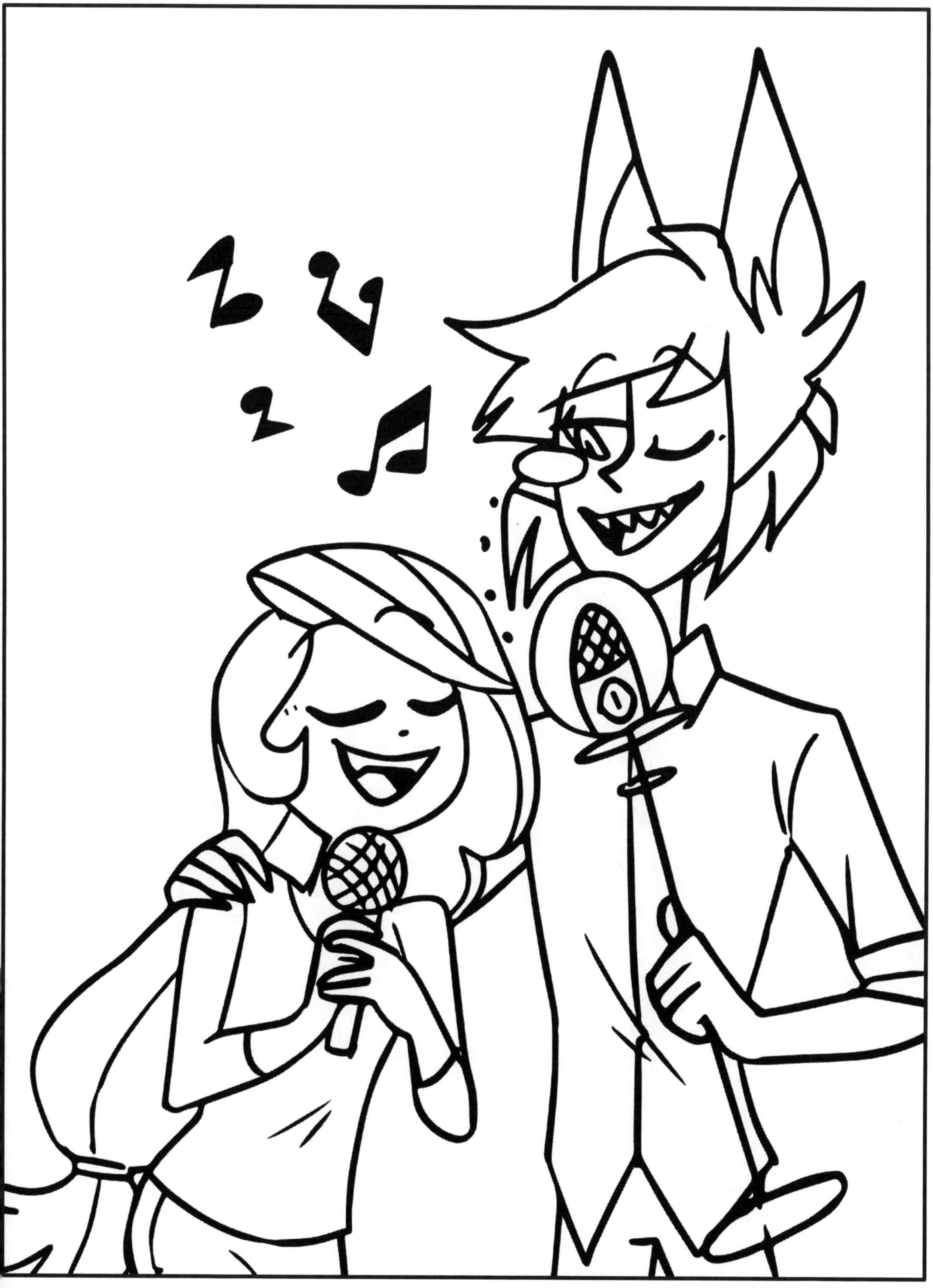

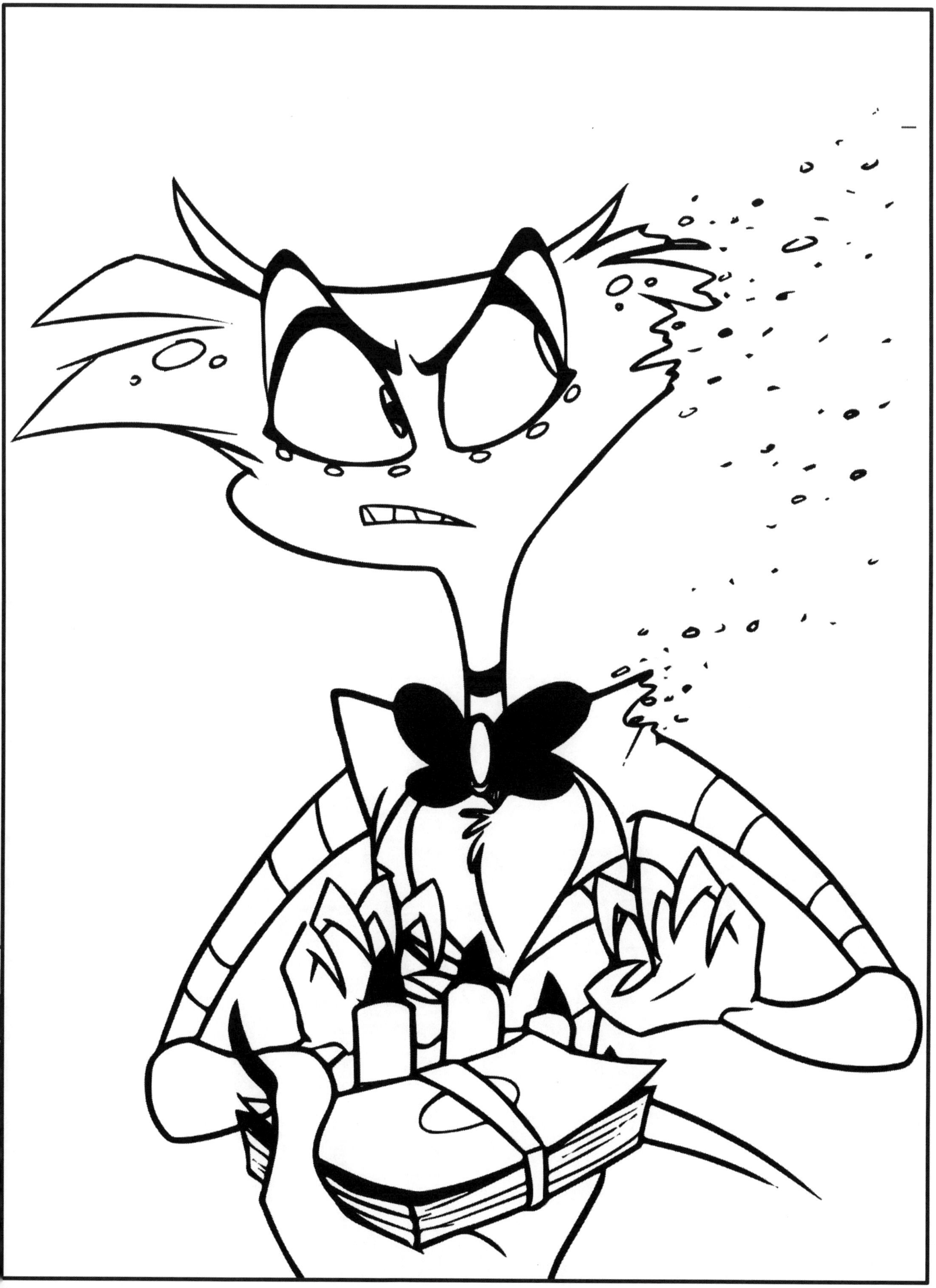

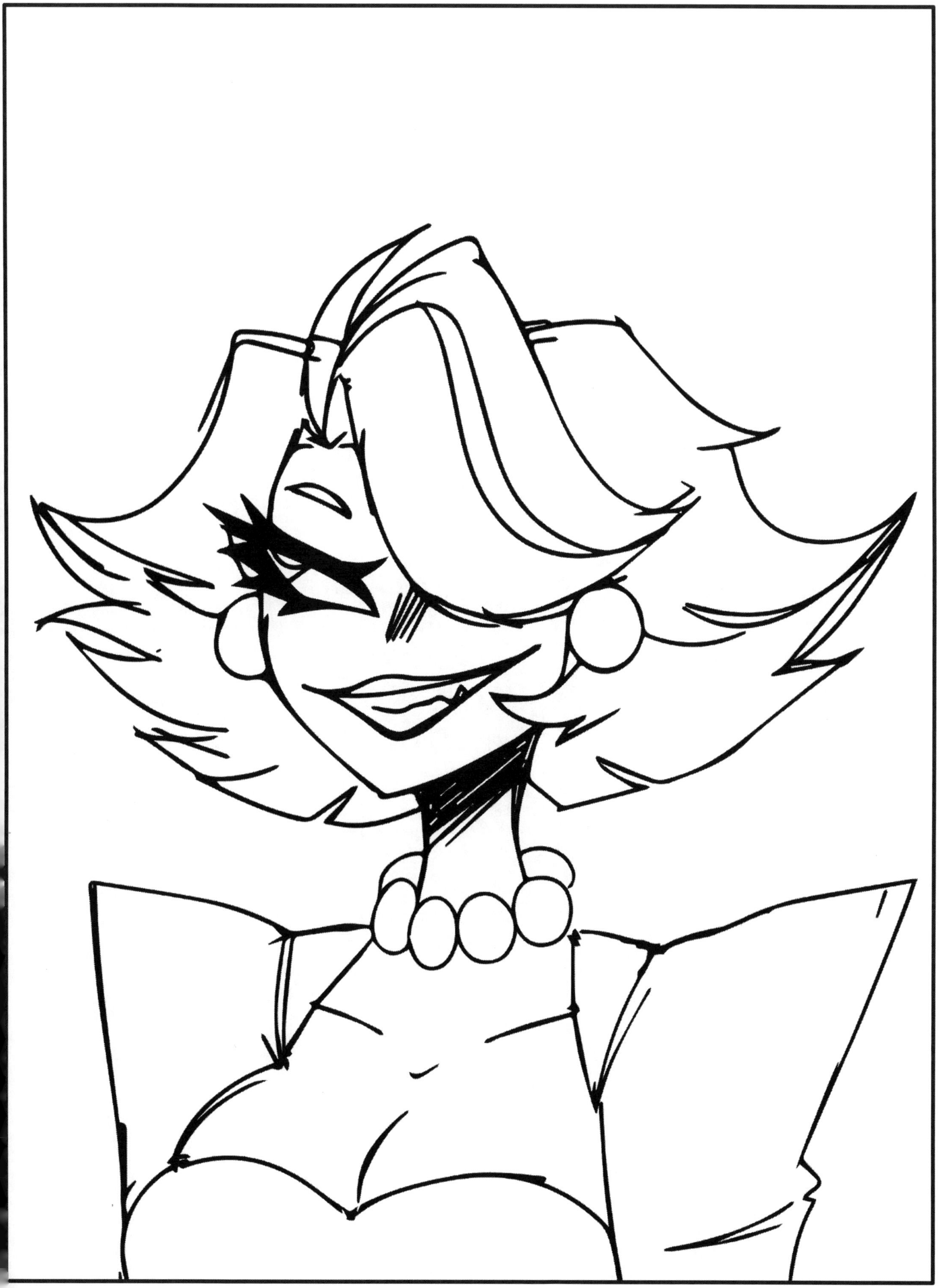

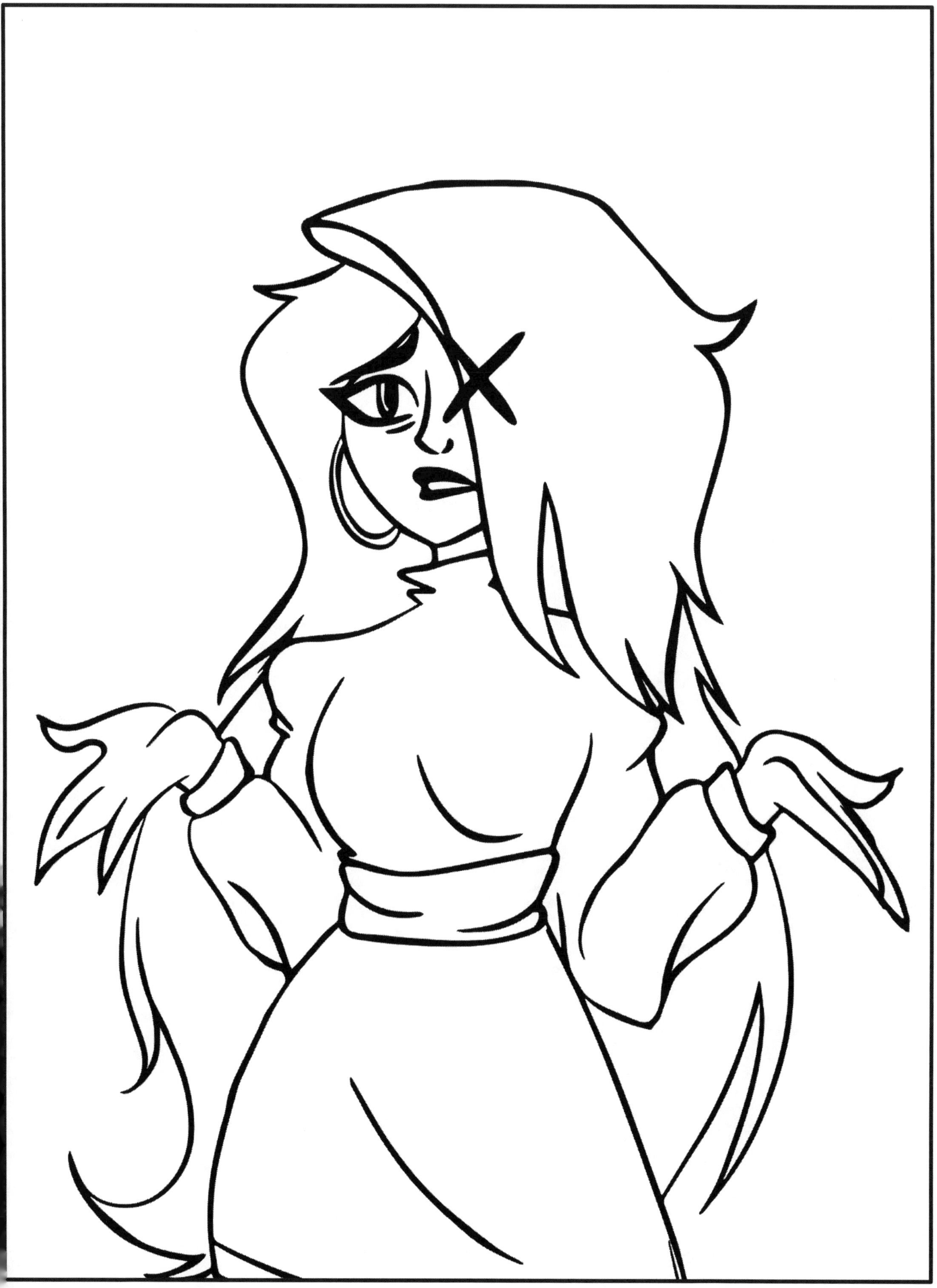

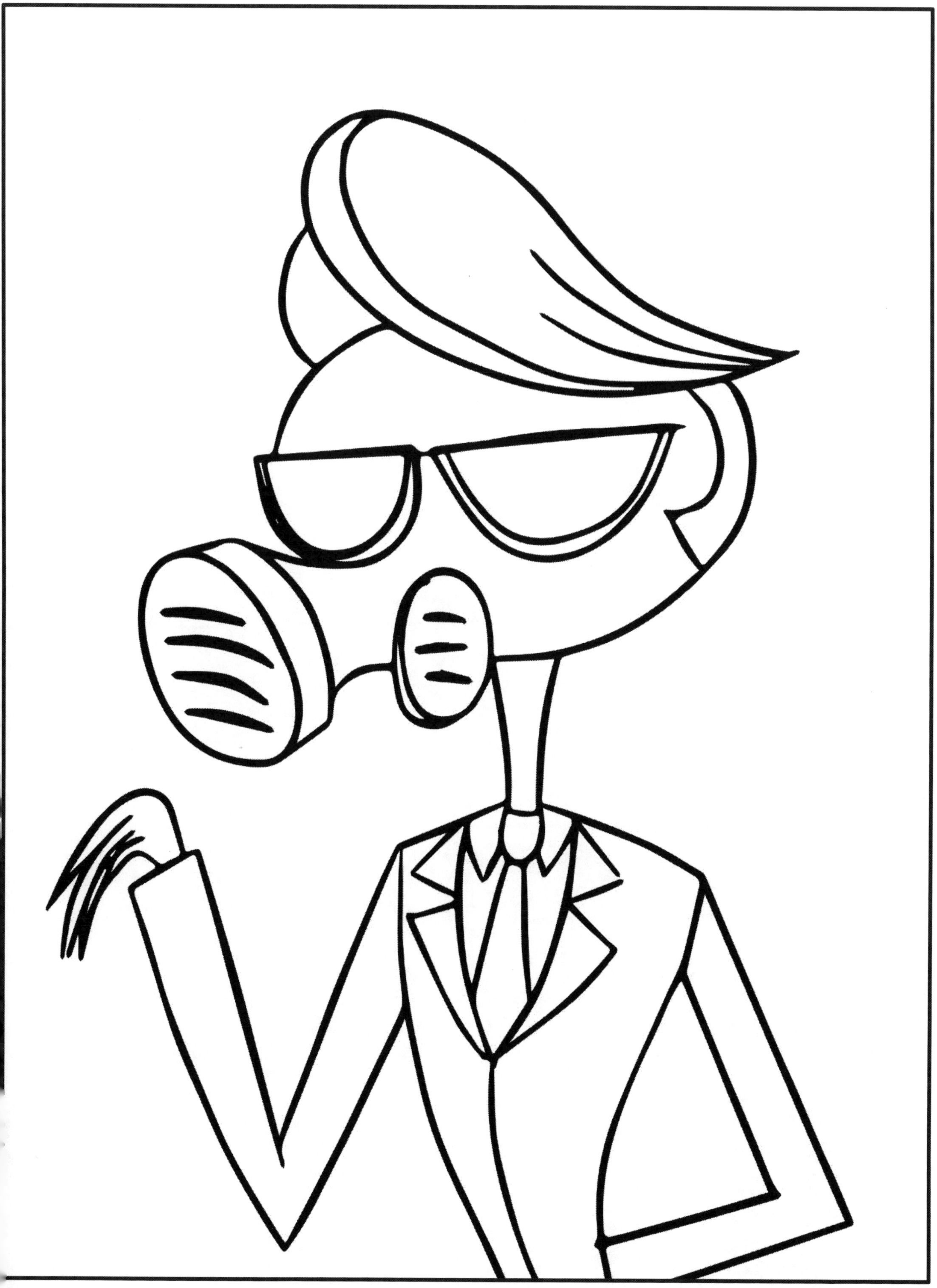

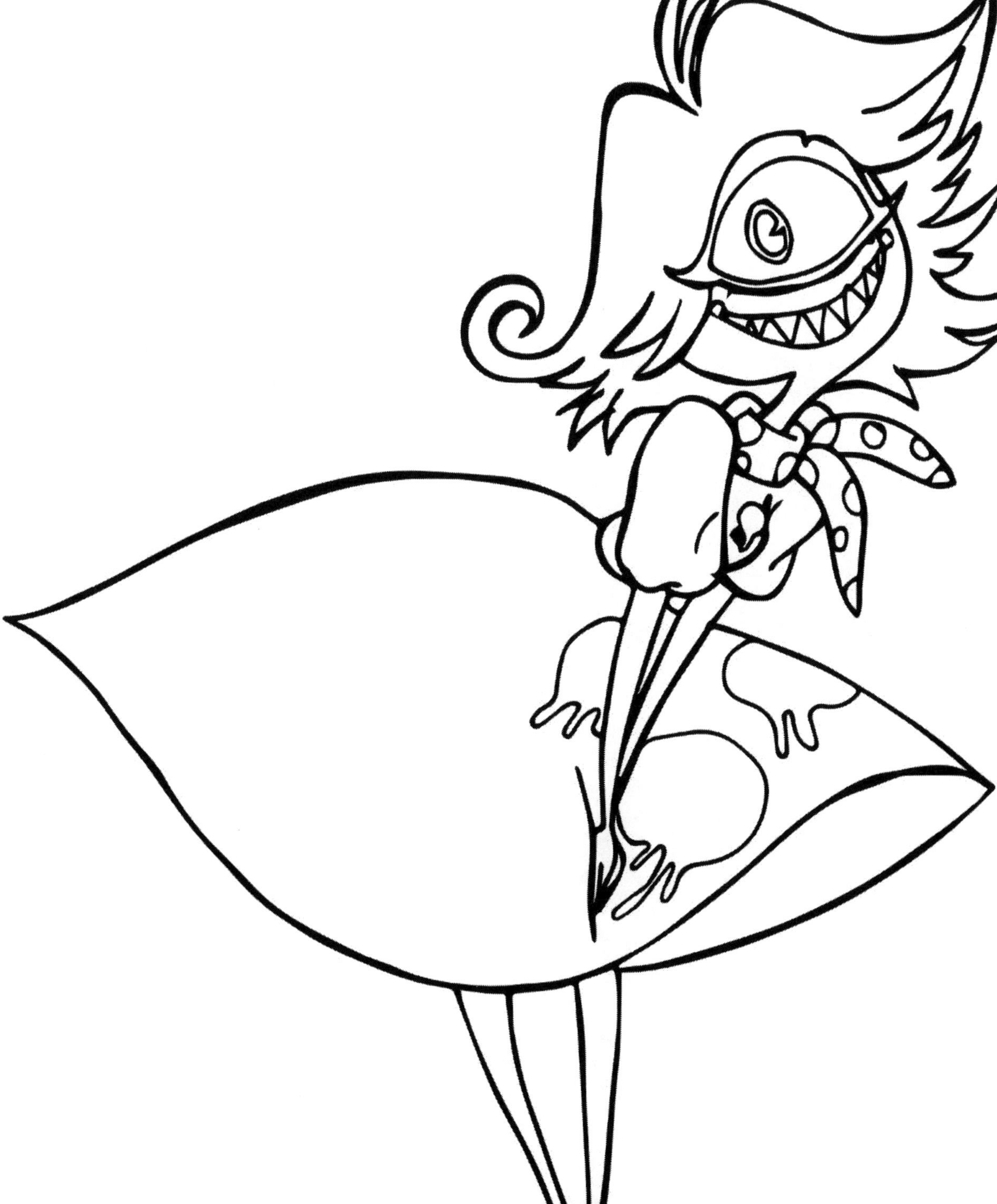

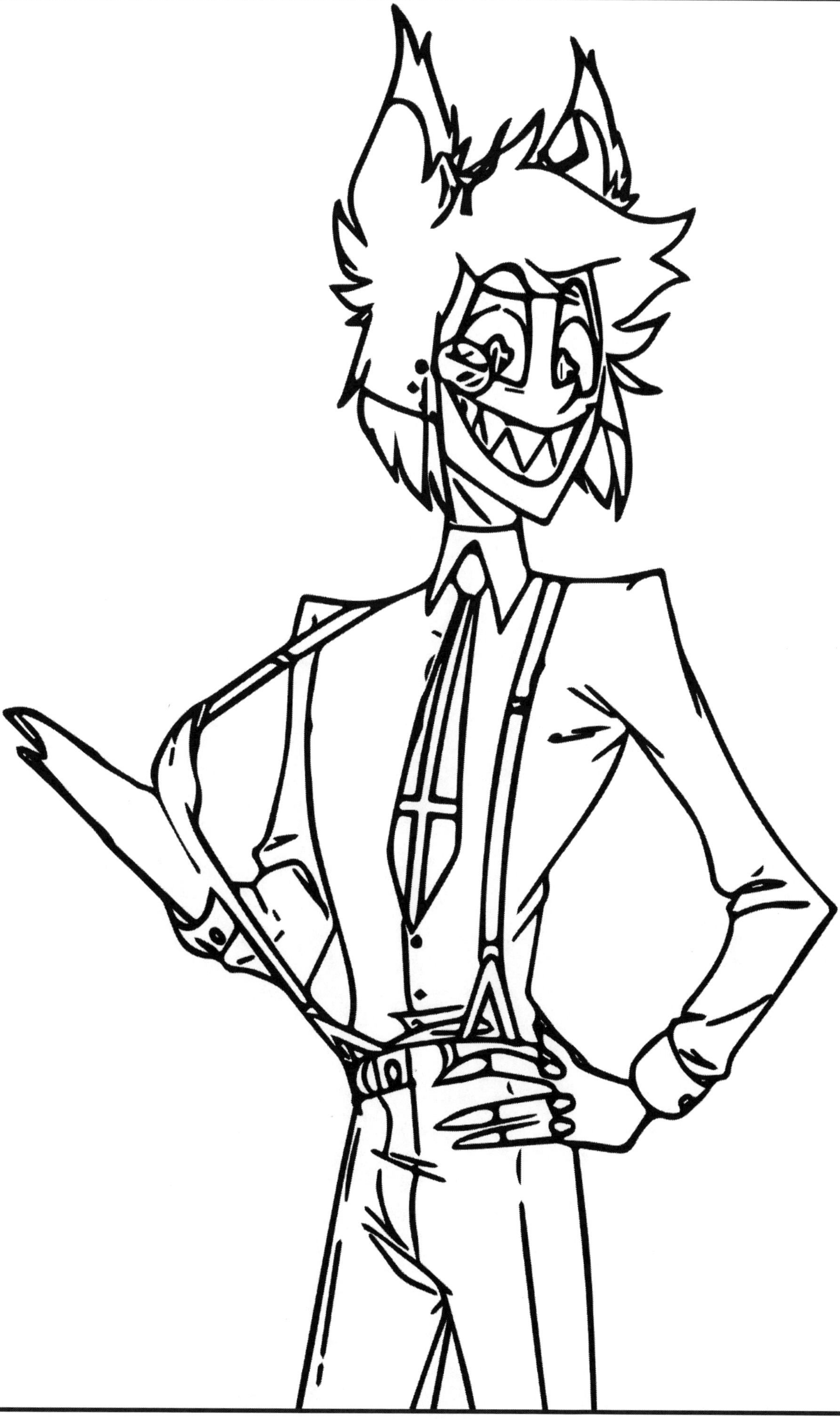

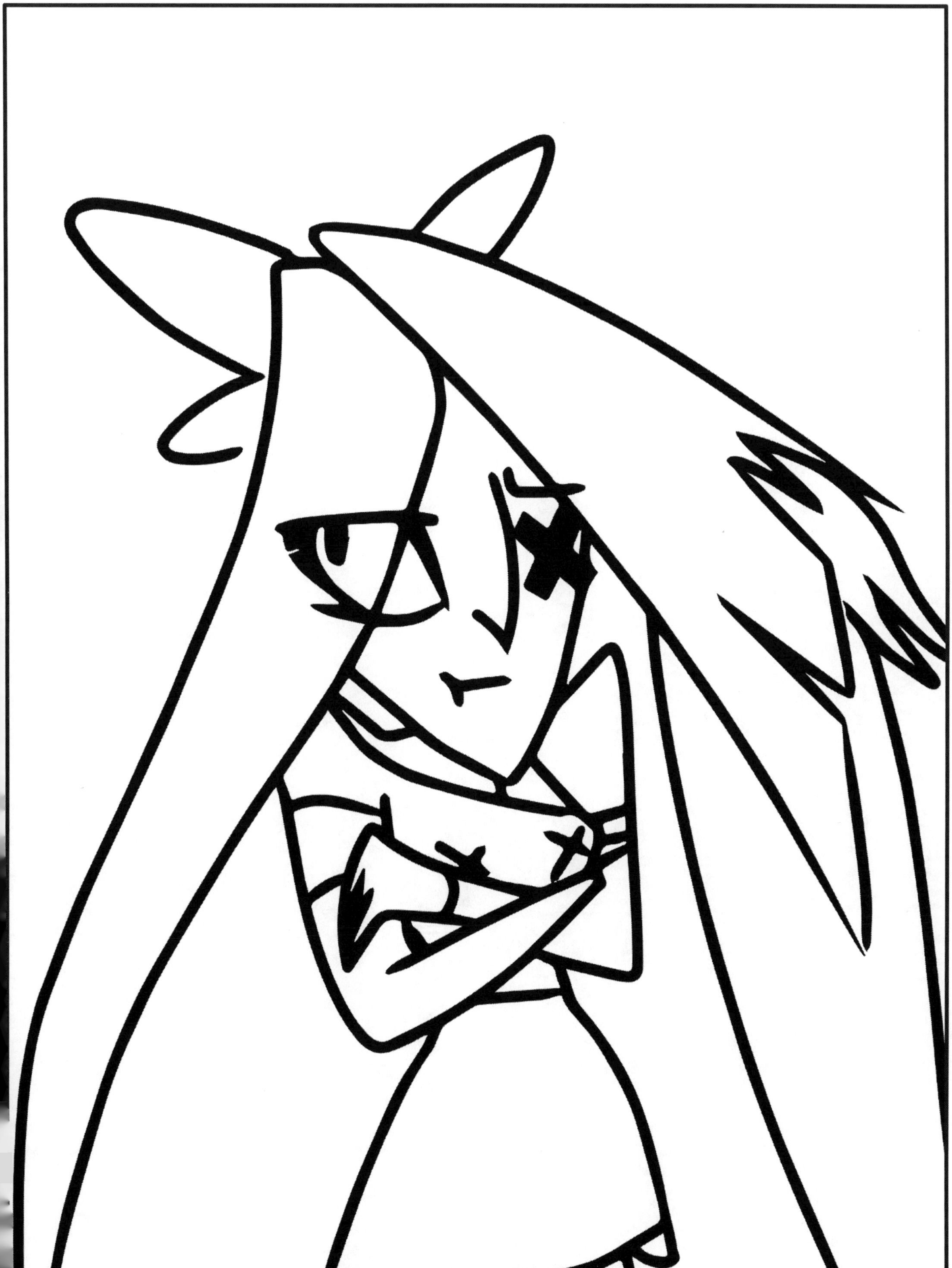

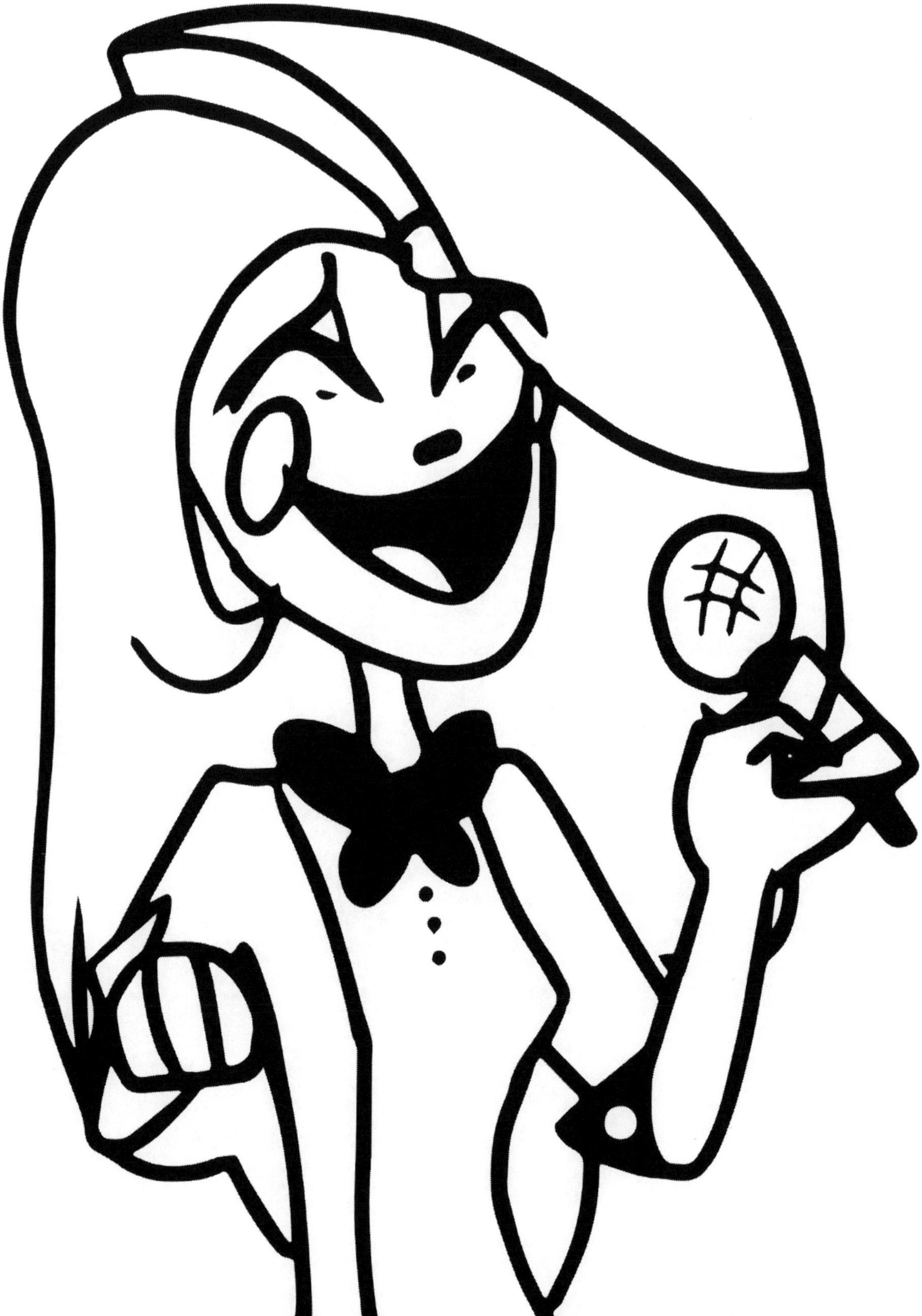

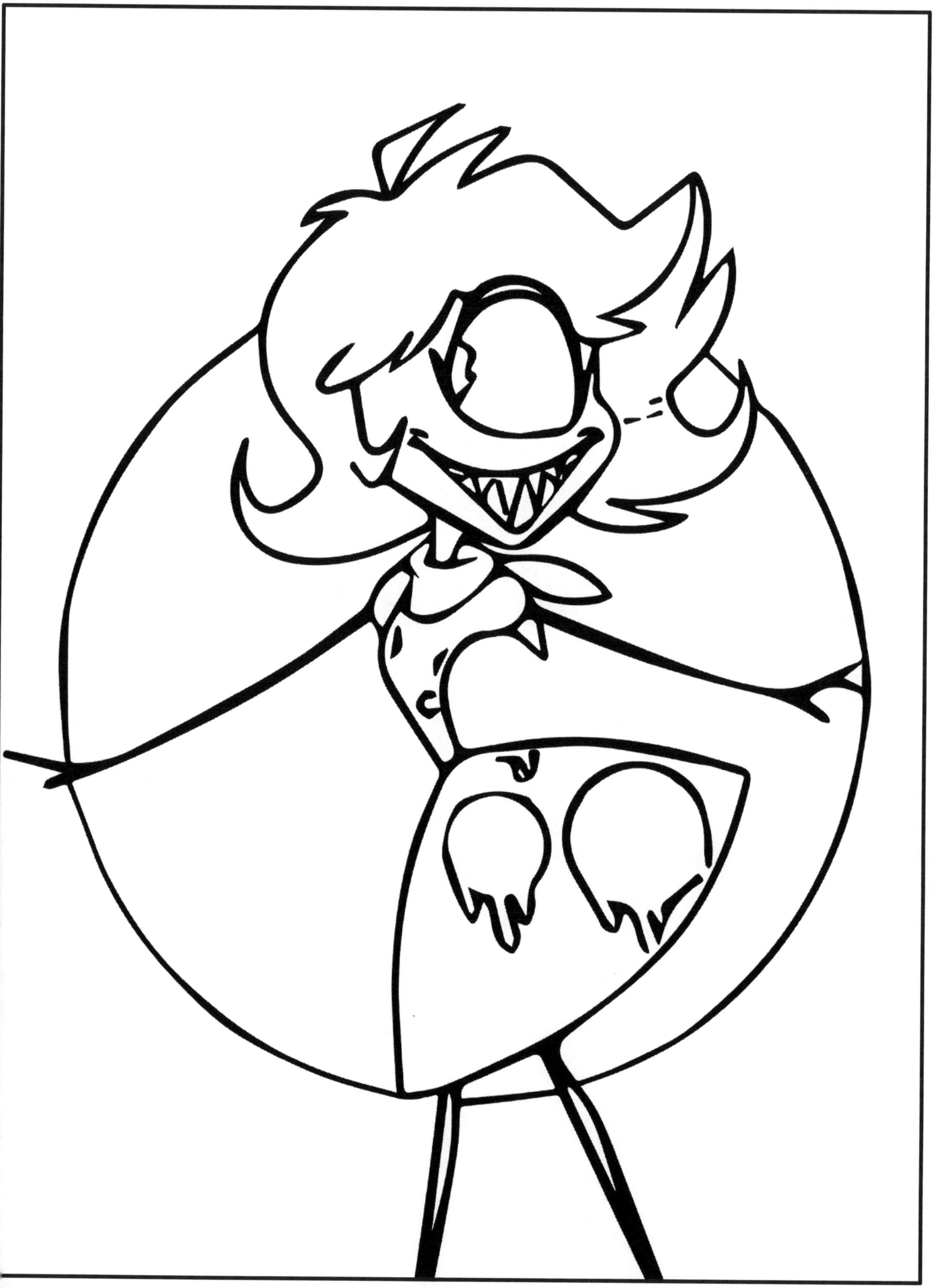

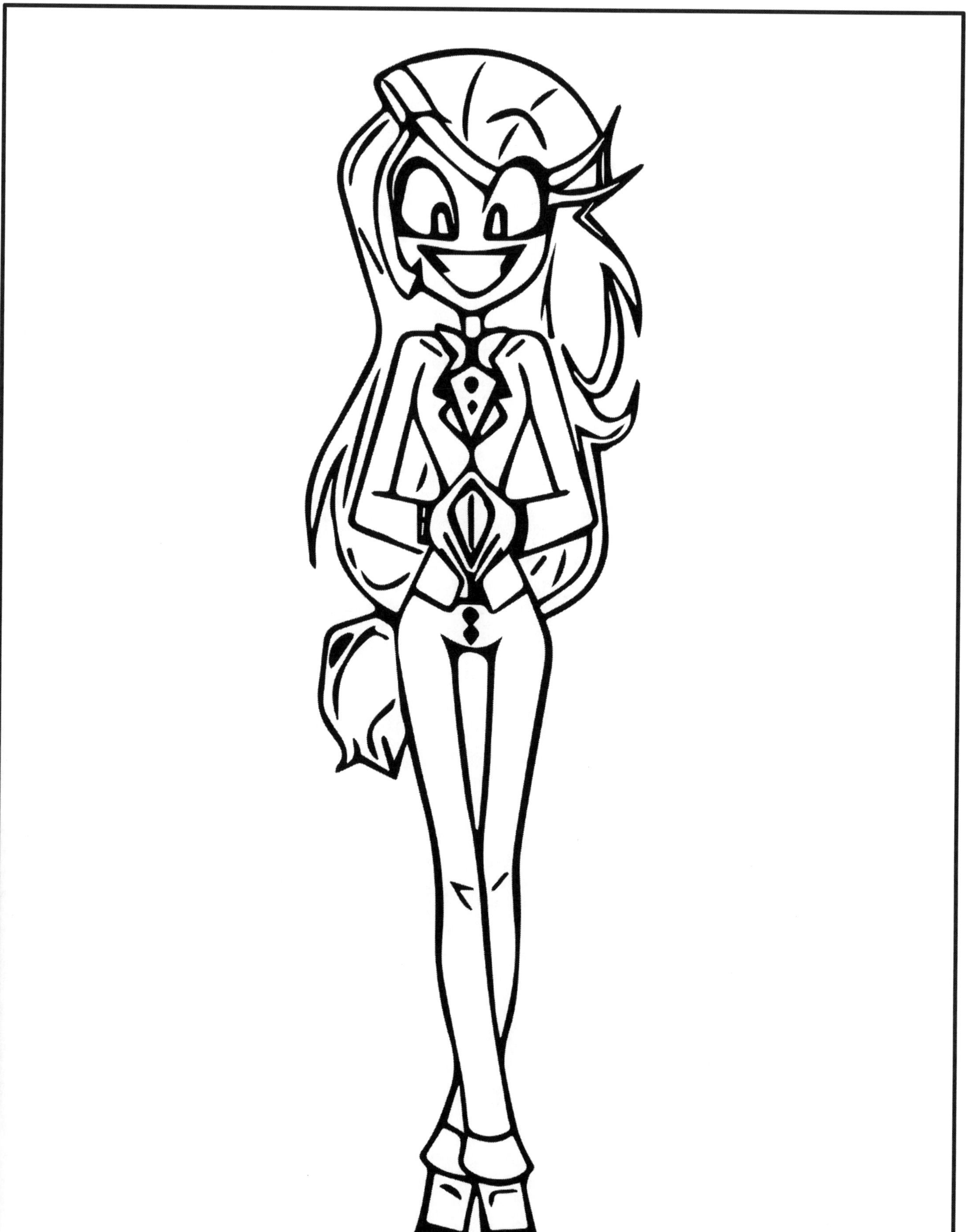

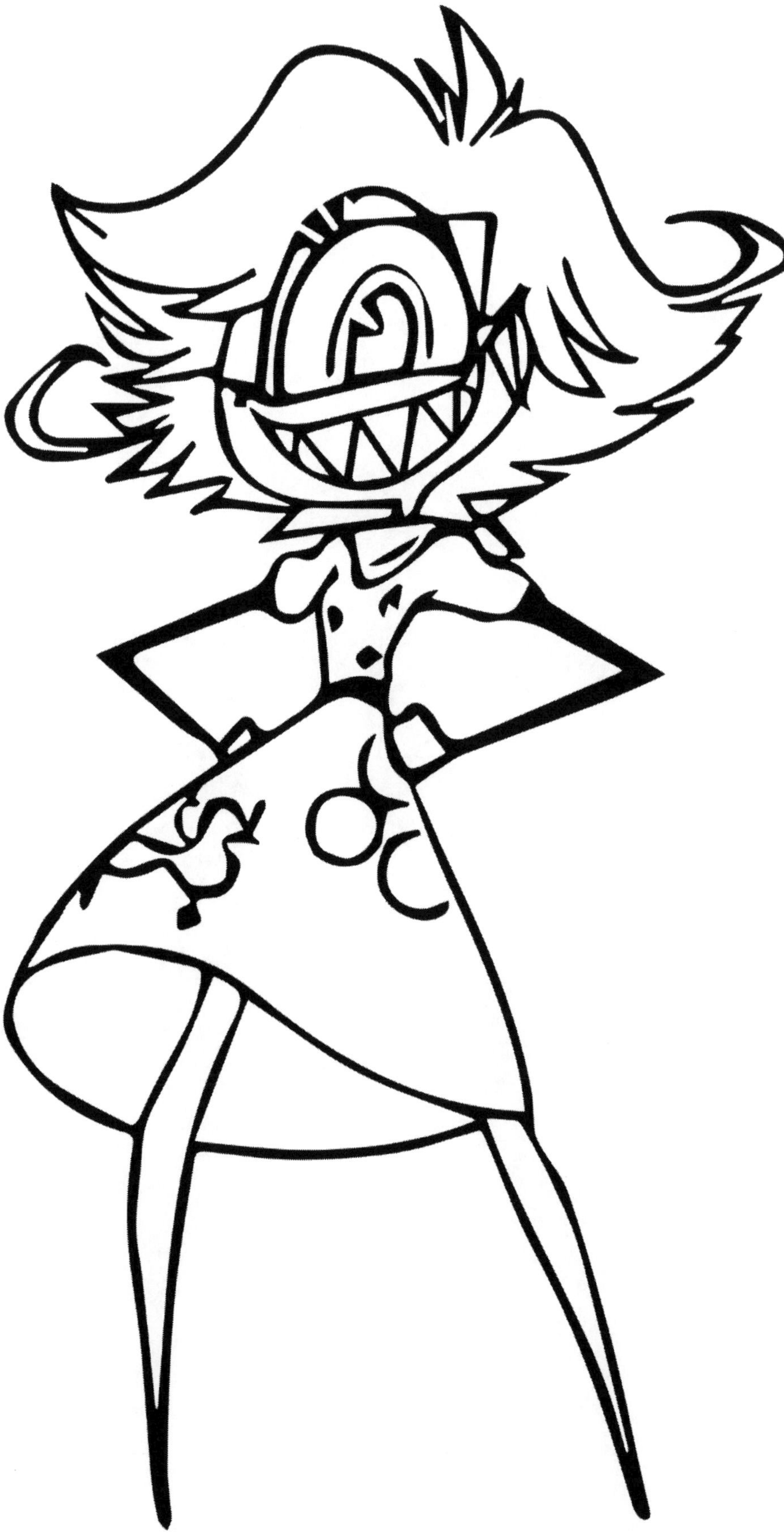

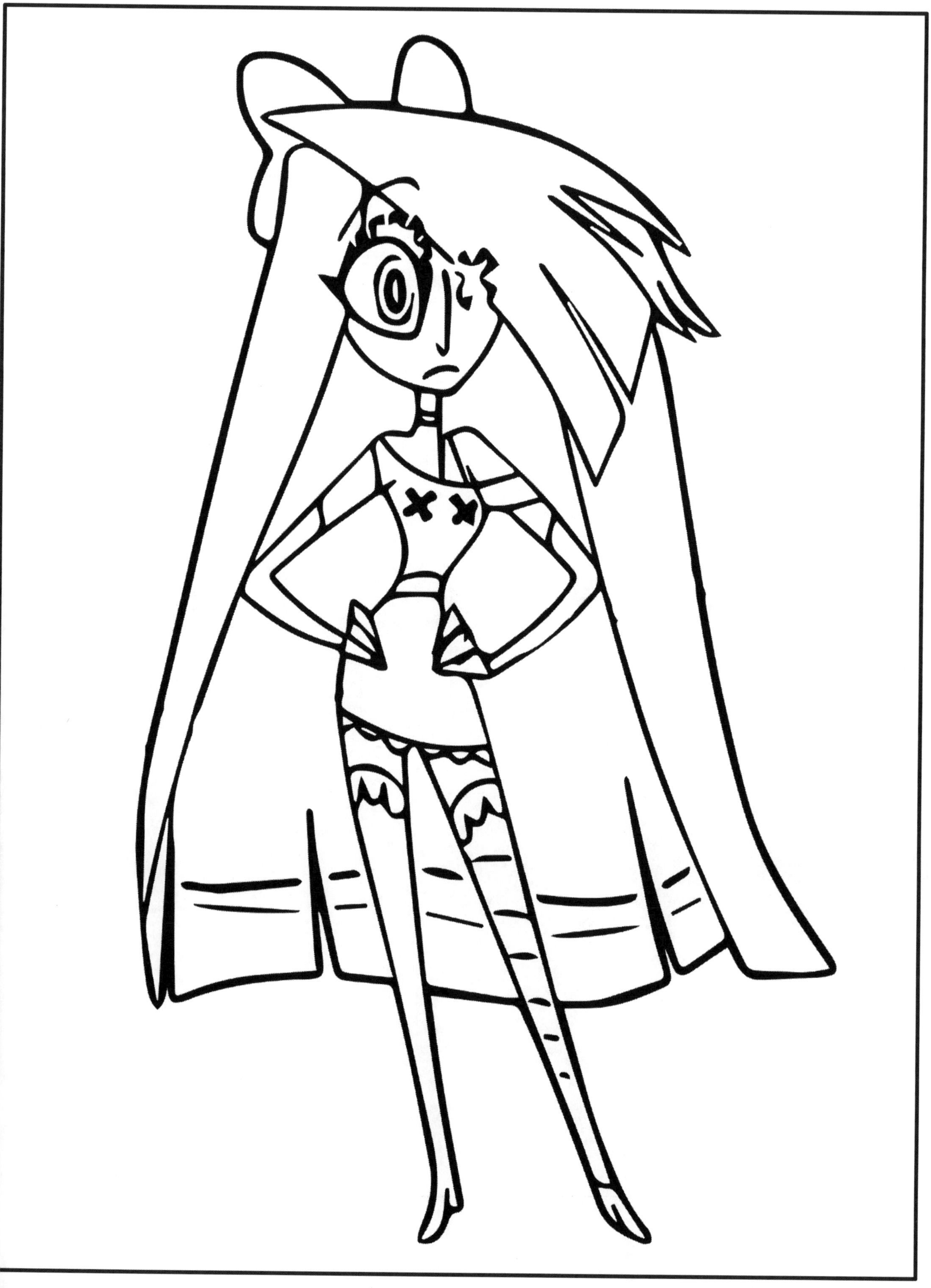

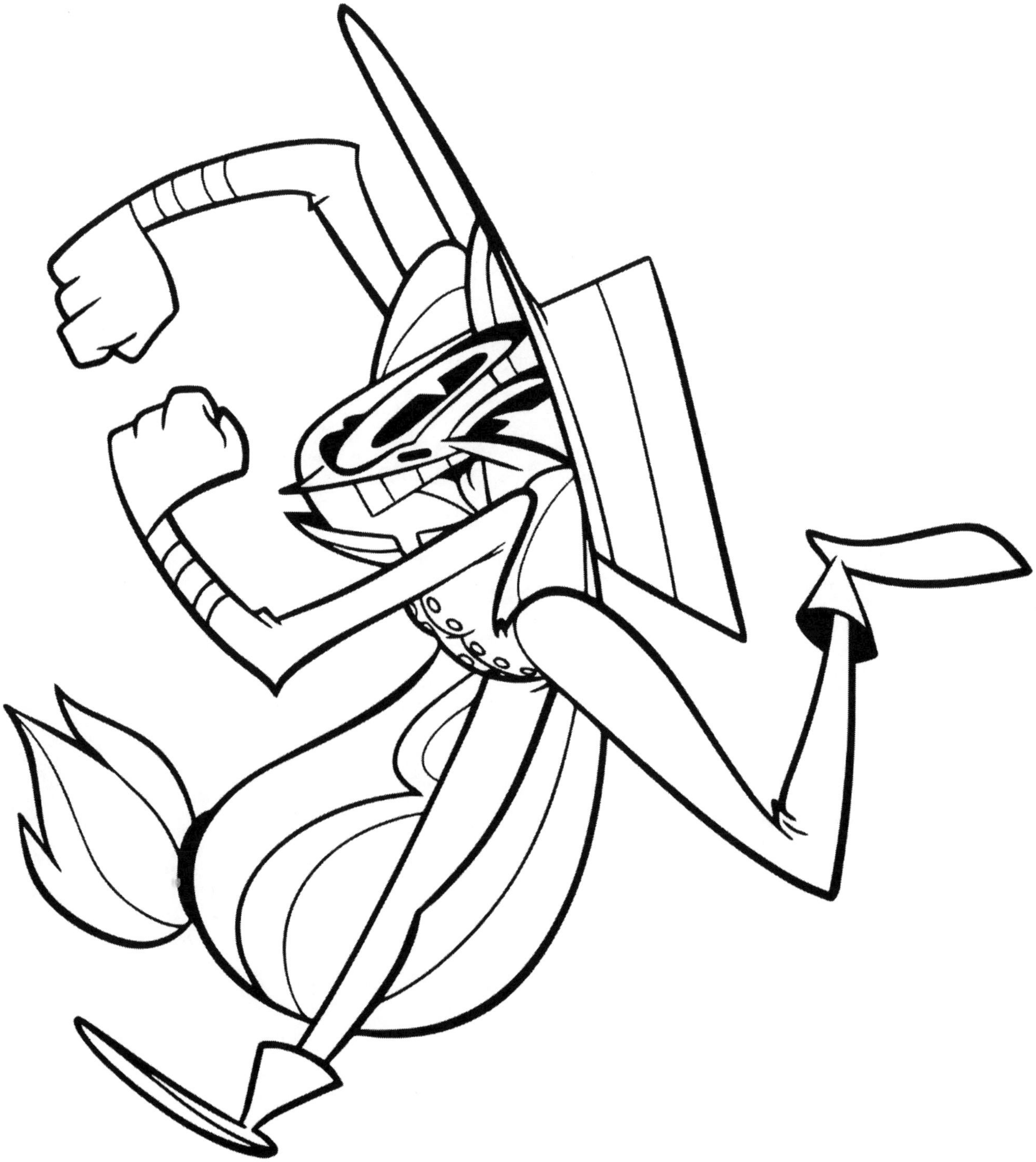

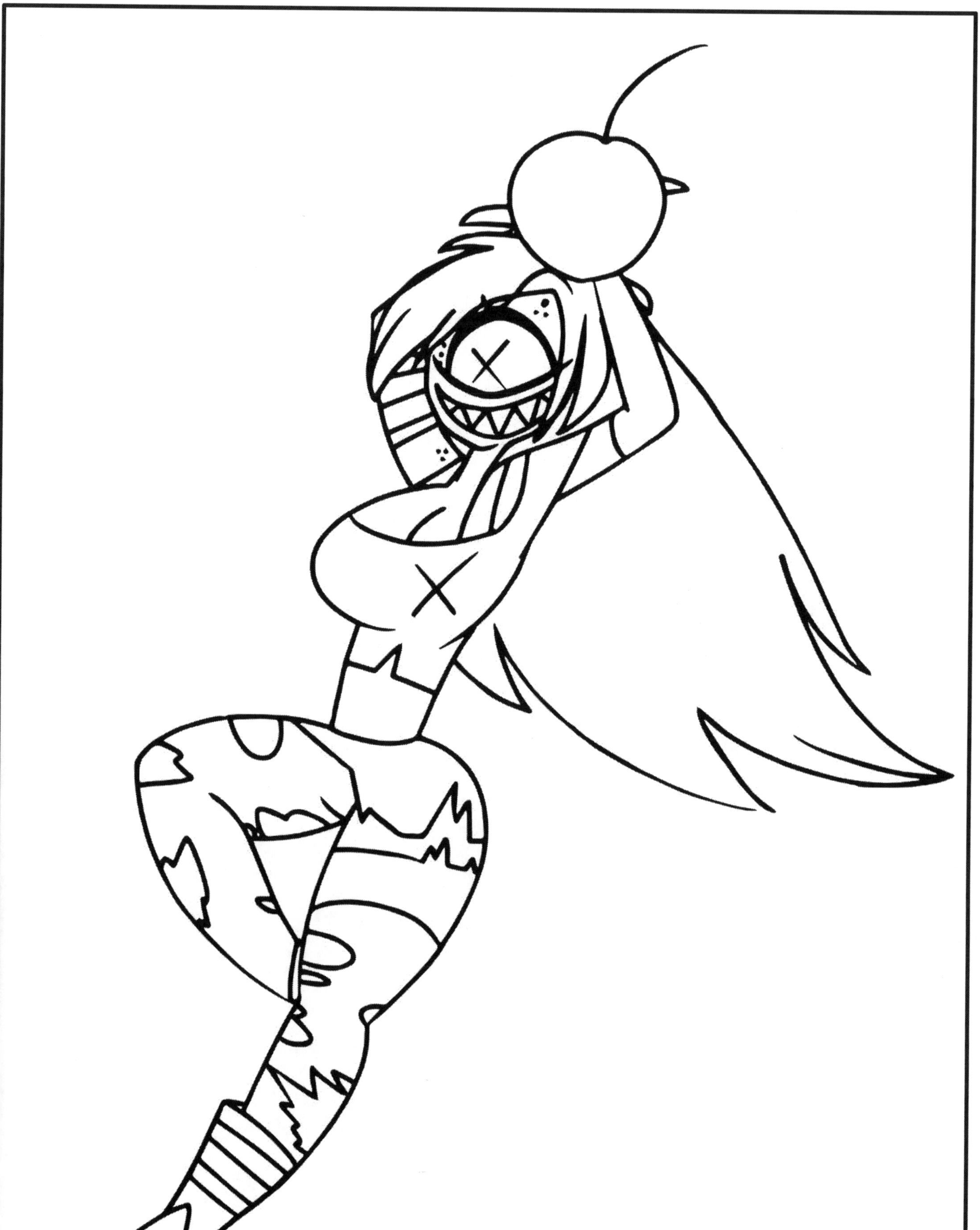

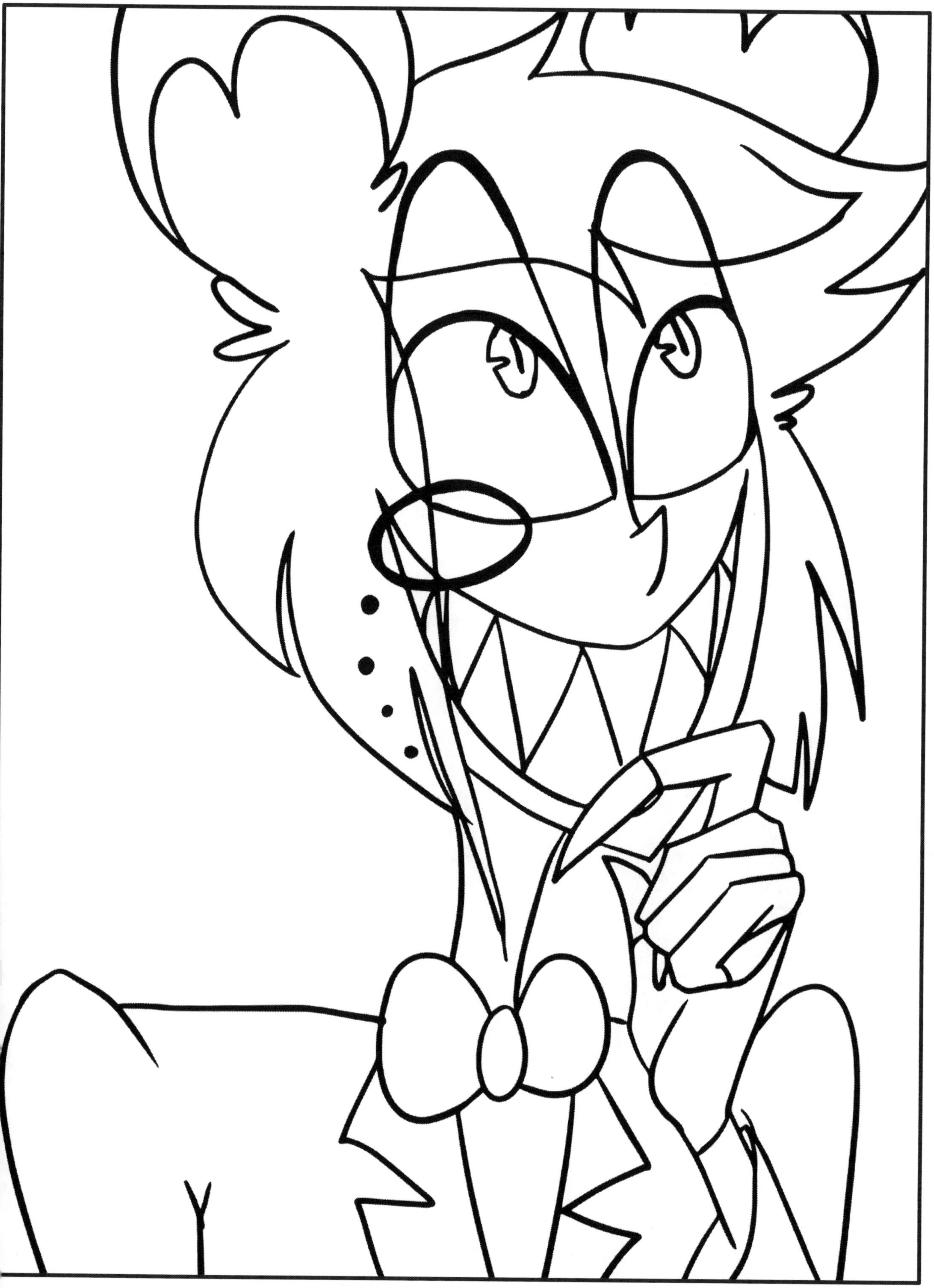

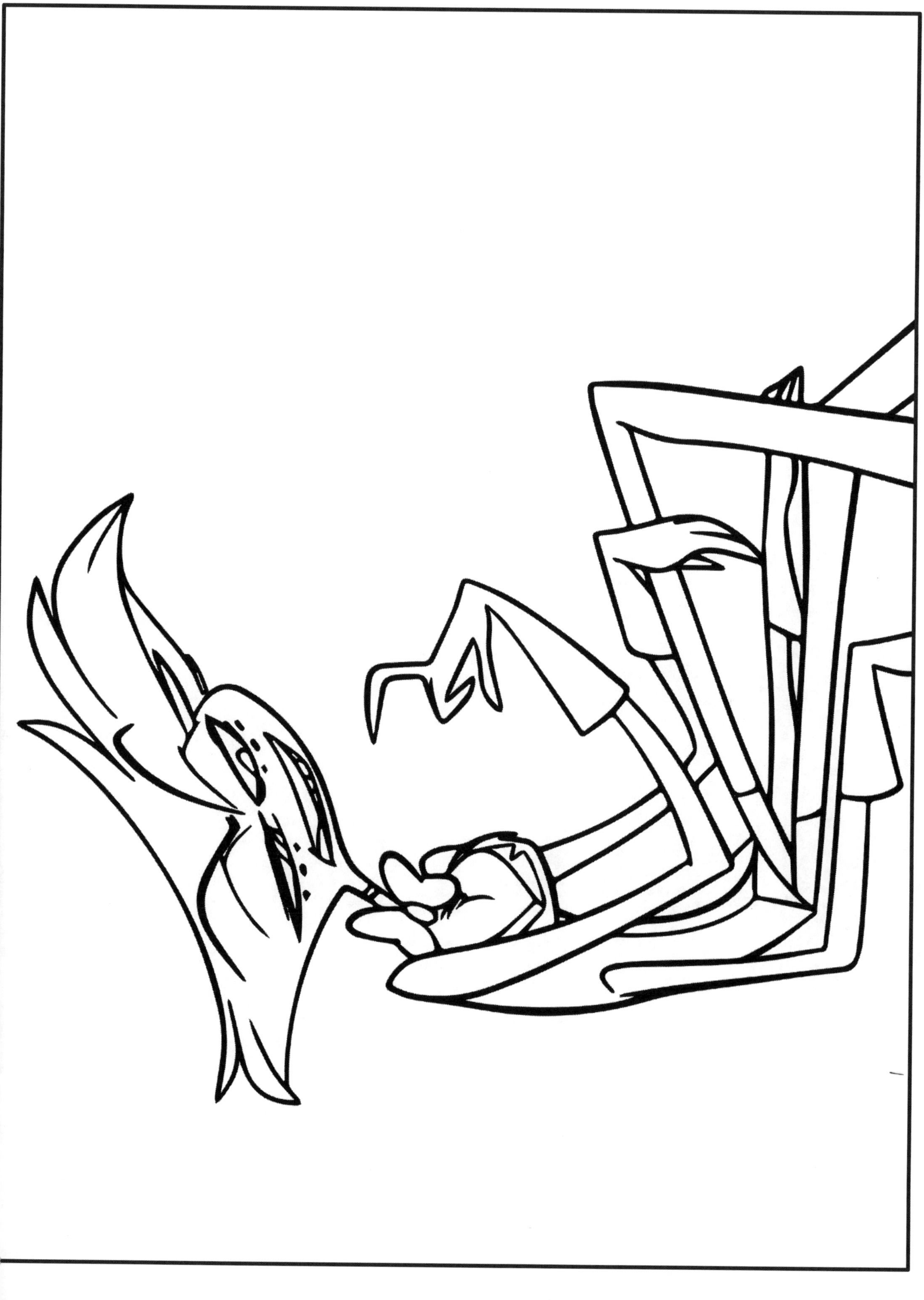

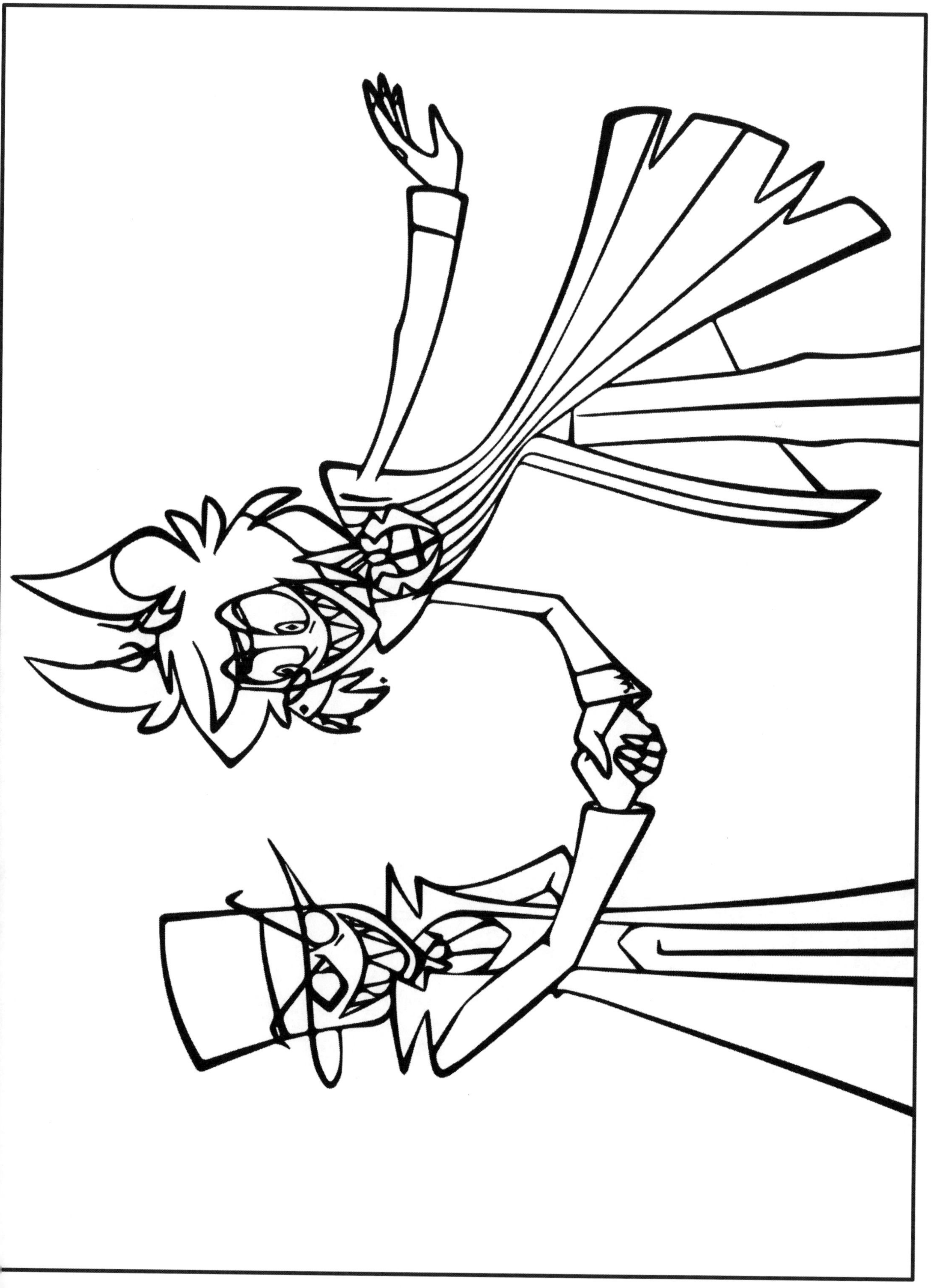

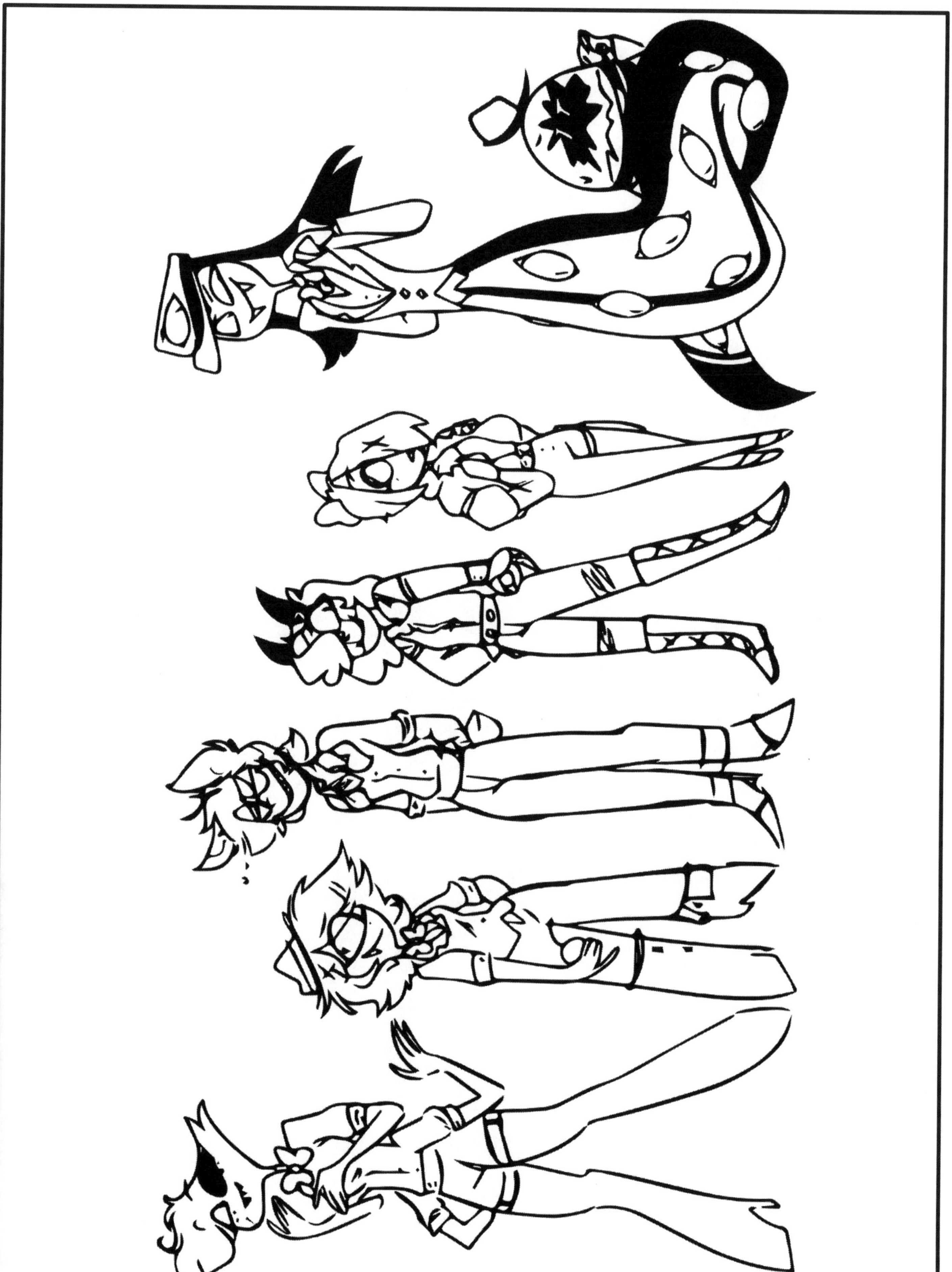

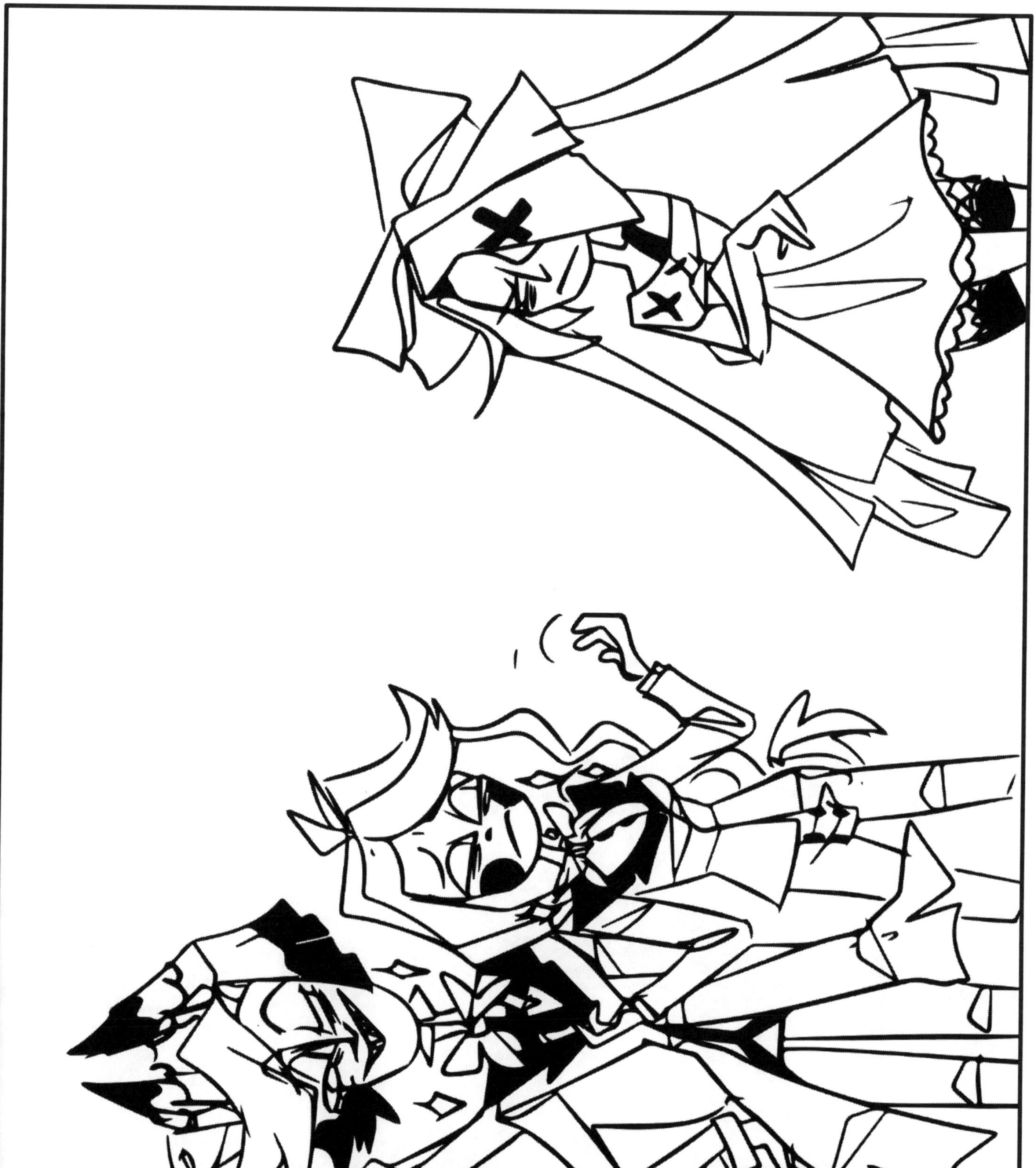

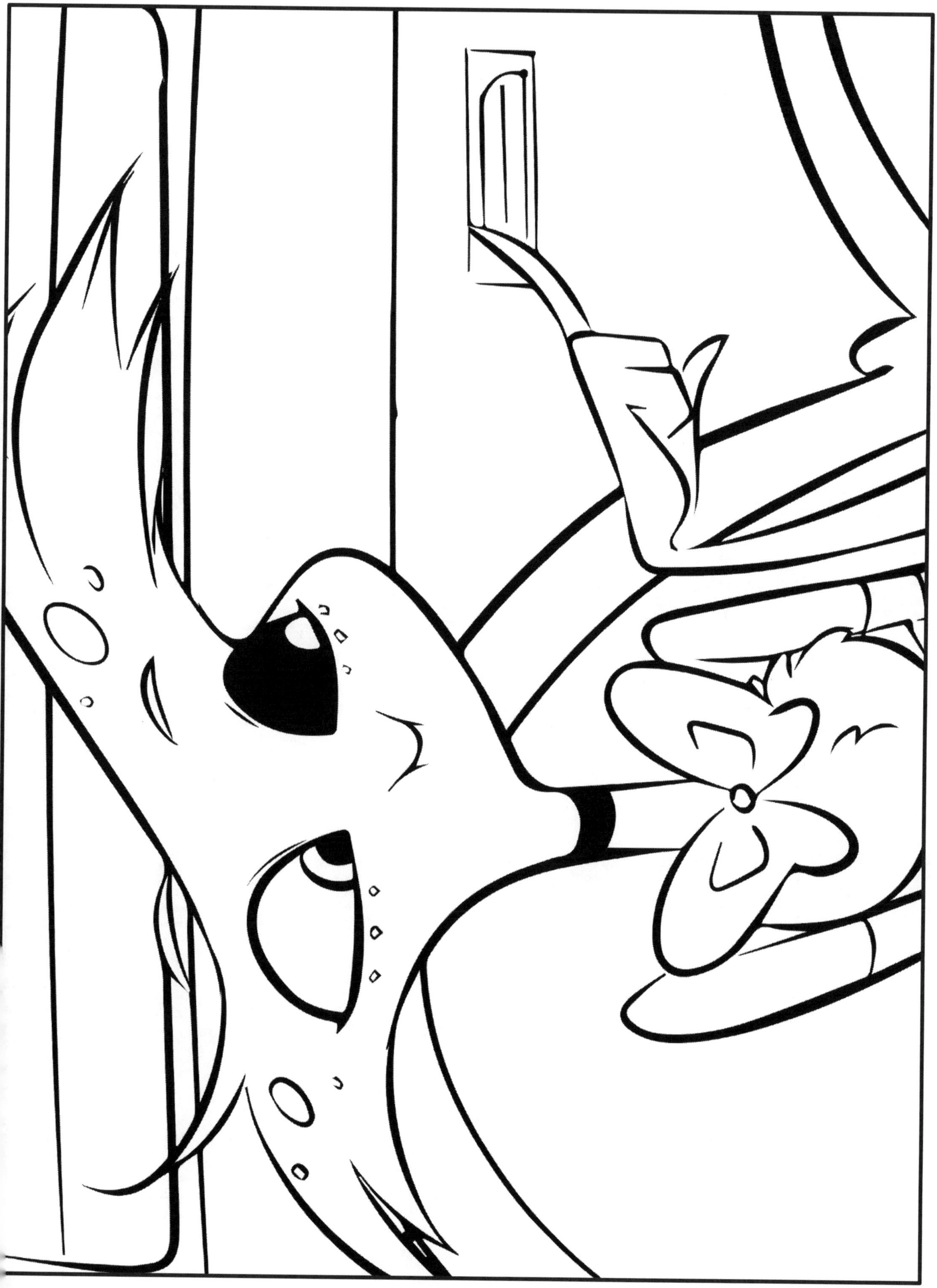

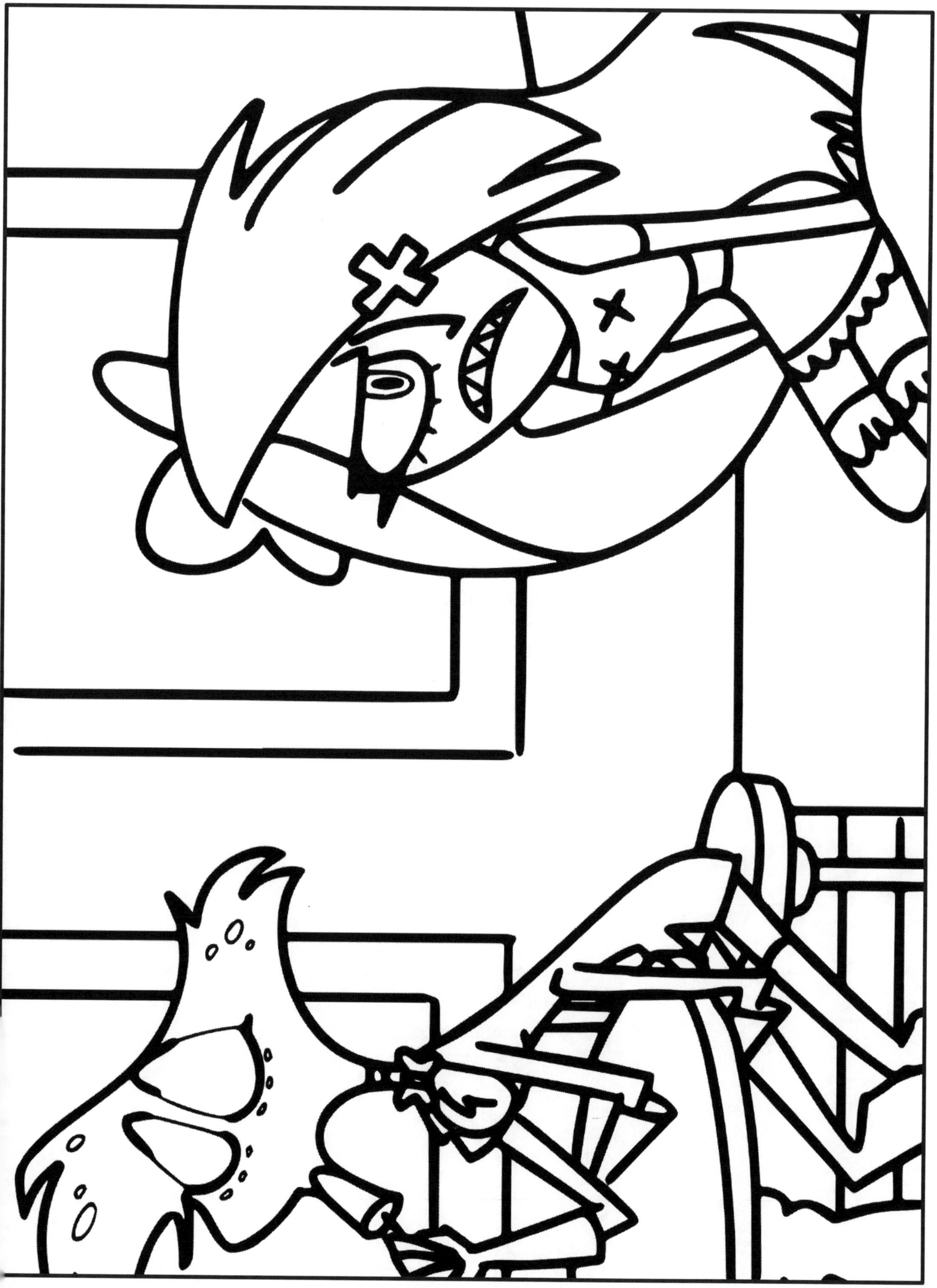

Made in the USA
Middletown, DE
30 September 2023

39846734R00035